M.O.M.

M.O.M.

Moments of Motherhood

LAWANDA GHOLAR

Superior Publishing LLC.

Contents

To the loves of my life, my husband and children, I love you and thank you for allowing the world a glimpse of our lives.

To my mom, Martha, your love and prayers have gotten me to this point and I thank you for everything.

To Aunt Ethel and my late Aunt Deneise, thanks for the love and support.

To all the moms that spend countless hours loving, providing, and praying; you are awesome. To the ladies that may not have the title of mom, but you do the things that moms do; you are appreciated.

God gets the glory.

Copyright © 2022 by LaWanda Gholar

ISBN:9781953056351
ISBN:9781953056313

Copyright © 2022 COVER DESIGN, NICORRI THOMAS-BROWN

All rights reserved. No part of this book may be reproduced in any manner whatsoever without written permission except in the case of brief quotations embodied in critical articles and reviews.

SUPERIOR PUBLISHING LLC, JULY 2022
CEDAR BLUFF, MS 39741
(662) 295-9893

Have you ever met someone that is just kind and doesn't require anything in return, just a friendship? (Journal about your friendship)

September 2, 2021

Count it all joy. God is merciful and his grace is enough. It is good when people think about you. Today I was gifted with this notebook/journal. My coworker gave it to me. She has always been so kind and thoughtful. Her attitude towards situations are one of a kind. She loves and gives wisdom. It is truly a blessing to have her as a friend, co-worker, sister in Christ. She has other people's interest at heart and can sometimes put herself to the side. I am thankful for her and because of her, I continue to have a great friendship with her daughter who once was my coworker but is a great friend. Her daughter is similar to her and I don't think she realizes just how much. It is just a blessing to meet wonderful, loving people.

Have you ever had a game plan that didn't work as you thought? How did you tackle it?
(Journal your thoughts)

September 10, 2021

On Saturday, September 4, 2021, at Veterans Memorial Stadium, my son's journey to the NFL took a detour. He had about 50 yards with 8 carries against the opponent. In the 3rd quarter he ran for 15 yards and was tackled in the right ankle. They pulled him out of the game. After we made it home from the game he said he felt that he disappointed us because of his injury, especially because he had an aunt and uncle that traveled from Texas to see him play. He felt ashamed because he didn't get to perform like he planned. He had his own cheering section. I had to assure him that what happened was beyond his control and no one in our family was disappointed, that we were all cheering him on because he was playing so well.

We found out on Tuesday, September 7, 2021 that he had a broken ankle. The 2nd game of the season and he was out with an injury for the rest of the year. Just like that! We were hoping for just a sprain because he worked so hard for the past year and a half. He changed from defense to offense during the spring, so we were anticipating a great year! Wednesday, September 8, 2021 he had surgery. He said his surgeon performed surgery on an NFL player in his younger years while he was in high school or college, I can't recall which. The surgery went well. It lasted about an hour. Before he went into surgery, even though he was a little loopy, he remembered his coach telling him they wished him well. He loves his team and respects his teammates and coaching staff.

Today, Friday September 10, 2021 is game day. Our team takes on a local team. He was so ready for this game. As soon as he saw the schedule, he was super excited because he was going to have the opportunity to play against a few of his former teammates from his little league team.

Of all days to take team pictures, they took pictures prior to today's game. This is his first game not playing. When he found out about this and he wasn't able to participate, he felt like he wasn't part of the team. I know, this may seem minor, but when your dreams seem to become out of reach right before your eyes; it's not so minor. We talked about it after he got the news of the photo shoot and he decided that he would show up to the game to let his teammates know that he was still a member of the team and was going to support them. When we made it to the field, the team was just unloading the buses and heading into the field house. The hugs and handshakes from his teammates and coaches is what he needed. He was super excited, scooter and all!

As the game was being played, I watched him on the sideline. He was coaching and encouraging the team. I know it had to be difficult seeing the team play, knowing that there was no way he could physically help them on the field. As his biggest fan, it was hard to see him on the sideline, not being able to play and contribute. After the game, he mentioned how he wished he could have helped the team. He also saw some areas the team could improve on. This time off will give him a chance to do what his cousin told him. He told him to look at the film from when he played last season and going forward and study EVERY position defense and offense.

I can remember him being this 5 year old, energetic boy that asked to play football. We used to live across from a high school. There was a team practicing on the high school practice field, but it wasn't the high school team. It was a little league team. From that year on, he has been playing football. I must say that this team set the foundation and allowed him the experience he needed to become the player he is now. He had awesome coaches from the time he started, until the time he left. His dad was also his coach for at least two years. I remember one game when he was playing with the little league, he played running back. There was a play where he was handed the ball and he ran for a touchdown. I was running right beside him on the sideline. He often brings this moment up maybe because he was excited that he scored and a little embarrassed by my shenanigans. At the time he played little league football I was the cheer-leading coach of the same team; this gave me the opportunity to be on the sidelines and I could cheer or coach(whichever was necessary) and he would definitely hear me. I haven't figured out how I can be on the sidelines during his high school years. He said to please not try because he knows I will talk to his teammates and he doesn't want me to embarrass him.

As a parent and as an educator, I wanted him to focus more on academics. Making it to the NFL is his dream, it's his Plan A. His dad and I have supported his dream from the beginning. He knows who his Savior is and he knows his football talents come from God. I remember we were riding in the truck one day and gospel singer, Jonathan McReynolds' song was on the radio. He said "Momma if God blessed me to have a voice like that, who knows where I'd be". Then he thought about it and said, "God has blessed me. He blessed me with the talent to run and be good at football." He mentioned that he knew he needed to remain humble.

September 13, 2021

My son didn't mind me returning to work. I've been home since his surgery. I didn't feel like leaving him alone, but I had to return to work. It was not an easy decision to make. It was a decision that I had to make. During the time I was at home with him, he was very adamant about only taking his pain medication when absolutely necessary. He was worried about the meds becoming addictive. I had to remind him that I was going to abide by the prescription. I did understand his concern. He was more concerned about the side effects of the medication rather than the benefits of the medication. Before he would take any medication, I had to tell him what I was administering to him. We think these children are not paying attention and are not concerned about real world situations........FALSE!

I had a breakdown this morning at work. Before I left for work; I snapped at my husband, cried, and screamed in the shower, questioned God and just really fell off the faith wagon. It was bad when I first got to work. I just cried! I know that God is a healer and provider and that all things happen with his permission. If I could trade places with my son, I would. After all the tears my coworkers assured me of God's grace and mercy.

I got myself together and had a great day. I guess I just had to release my worries externally. I didn't tell my mom what happened, but I told my aunt. I just didn't want my mom to worry about me. I had to apologize to my husband because I was not so nice this morning. With God's covering, I made it!

When I arrived home he was on the sofa. He had completed some school assignments, but had not eaten. There was no reason for him not eating because I cooked breakfast and placed it inside a container so he could carry it. I also had lunch and a snack available. I don't know why he didn't eat, I can't worry about it. I did my part. When his sister made it home from school she spent time with him; and of course she did what sisters sometimes do, AGGRAVATE him!

September 14, 2021

Today he returned to school. I was so worried about him. You know, children in high school can be so mean and hateful. But he is a trooper. He has a personality of "it's about me, not them." I pray that he didn't miss too much work and can make it up. Honestly, you would think that after what he has gone through that his teachers would just allow him to start from his return date of today with current assignments. I am almost certain this will not be the case.

I picked him up from school and he said he was offered assistance to get to his classes by his teammates and classmates. He didn't use the scooter often, he said it was just easier to maneuver with the crutches, for the most part.

September 18, 2021

About yesterday and last night, the football booster club had a tailgate at the school. The vendor had great service and the food "Oh my!" The food was delicious! I was happy that my son was in good spirits. I know he was wanting to play, but he still felt useful. During the game he was on the sideline cheering, coaching, and talking the guys up. He couldn't have been more supportive of the team in their victory;15-12. It was a GOOD game. Defense won this game, hands down! After the game, while in the truck he asked me why God allowed him to be injured. I wanted to tear up. I didn't have the answer he was probably looking for, but I told him God has a bigger plan that is beyond our understanding.

Sometimes walking while blind can be challenging.
How did you bounce back into believing?
(Journal your experience)

September 19, 2021

Currently, church is virtual. I normally view two services. Since services are online, it gives me the opportunity to leave one online service just in time for the next. I listened to the pastor of the first service and he talked about being humble and loving. These are traits that my husband and I have taught the children. I know that this will get you closer to where you want to be as well as where God needs you to be. The message that really hit home was from the second service. We were reminded that God is always with us. I felt for a moment that God had abandoned us. I thought, "Why did our kids have the injuries and have such a challenging time the past year and a half?'" My daughter broke her ankle the first Saturday in February 2020. I know I am not the only person that feels this way. You sometimes feel like you and your loved ones are the only ones going through obstacles. I remember when my aunt was battling her fight with cancer she would say "Why not me, I am not better than anyone else?" I am constantly learning how to activate my faith and not allow it to sway. Sometimes when you are in your time of hardship, you just feel alone and helpless, but we really are not.

September 23, 2021

    This morning I woke up to an old church song in my heart that we used to sing *"Just a Little Prayer"*. I didn't know why, but after speaking to my coworker, I know why that song was on my heart. People get sick, they get better, but some don't overcome their sickness. I know that I'm learning on this journey about faith building. I am trying to not show any emotions, but it's hard not to when you have endured what others are currently going through. It sometimes causes you to go through your experiences again mentally. I now stand on John 13:7 which reads: "Jesus replied, "You do not realize now what I am doing, but later you will understand."

September 26, 2021

    Today is Sunday. We've had a busy weekend thus far. My injured player went to the doctor on Friday to have his stitches removed. The doctor didn't do x-rays, but will on his next visit. He was super excited to have his stitches removed. He asked her about possibly playing the last two games of the season. She said she'd have to look at the x-rays to make that determination. We're being prayerful, but we don't want to rush it.

    Friday night the team played out of town. It was a good drive. My friend and former coworker rode with me and my daughter. My coworker is a book of knowledge and a great listener. She is an "open book" for those that she knows. The drive was good, but the game..... The defense for our team was unbelievable in the first half, they caused 3 turnovers! Our offense couldn't capitalize this game. I just want to see them more aggressive on both sides of the ball. I think sometimes they mentally defeat themselves by the hype surrounding the opponent. Personally, I feel that we are one of the best teams. I feel that anyone can be beaten on any game night. It's like my husband would tell our son, "You don't get prepared for a game the day of the game, but during the week". He always reminds him that the game has to be in you. (Like most parents).

September 26, 2021

Today is Sunday. We've had a busy weekend thus far. My injured player went to the doctor on Friday to have his stitches removed. The doctor didn't do x-rays, but will on his next visit. He was super excited to have his stitches removed. He asked her about possibly playing the last two games of the season. She said she'd have to look at the x-rays to make that determination. We're being prayerful, but we don't want to rush it.

Friday night the team played out of town. It was a good drive. My friend and former coworker rode with me and my daughter. My coworker is a book of knowledge and a great listener. She is an "open book" for those that she knows. The drive was good......

BUT THE GAME.....

The defense for our team was unbelievable in the first half, they caused 3 turnovers! Our offense couldn't capitalize this game. I just want to see them more aggressive on both sides of the ball. I think sometimes when we mentally defeat ourselves by the hype surrounding the opponent.. I feel that anyone can be beaten on any game night. It's like my husband would tell our son, "You don't get prepared for a game the day of the game, but during the week". He always reminds him that the game has to be in you.

I love the game of football. There were not many fans at the game supporting the team. The band was in attendance, but we didn't have any cheerleaders. So to pump the guys up, I led a few chants and the parents that were in attendance along with the band chimed in. Back to the game..... We are not consistent in blocking. One of his best friends had 3 sacks. He is pretty good. If the team would just let all their energy out on the field, we'd be unstoppable. I will support them to the end. I don't know the game as well as most, but I think our guys just need the support. If I knew the game like my husband, I'd be a football coach. Well, I think sometimes I already am because I coach from the stands.

Have you ever had to deal with grief? What got you through?
(Journal your progress)

September 29, 2021

Sometimes the place you don't want to be when going through a loss is the place you need to be. My students bring me joy and laughter. Monday when I was emotional, they showed me how much they cared. Today our family suffered a great loss. My husband doesn't know if he wants to release his grief or hold on to it. He's such a quiet, humble person. I understand how he feels, but we all handle grief differently. I just know I need to be there for him. When he's ready to talk, I'm here.

October 8, 2010, I lost my dad. He went into the hospital for surgery on Tuesday, October 5, 2010 to have a toe amputated. He never returned home. He died of aspiration. The day of his surgery, I was in his room when they wheeled him in from recovery. The nurse asked my dad if he knew me. He replied, "Yes, that's my bright and shining star." I stayed with him until later in the evening and I returned home. I called him every morning and night. On Thursday night, October 7, the kids sang "Nobody Greater Than You". He loved that song. Friday, October 8, I called him that morning on my way to work. He was still in the hospital. I called from the time I left home until the time that I made it to work. I never got an answer. I just assumed that something was wrong with the telephone lines. My dad was a person that would talk on the phone regardless of the time of day. I called again when I made it to work, no answer. It was almost 9 o'clock, right before we opened. I got a phone call from my brother. He said, "He's gone." I was so confused I didn't know what to do. My husband had to pick me up from work and drive me to my hometown. This was a day like no other. I felt like the world was caving in on me. There were so many things that I had to do that

I never thought about doing, like planning a funeral. My parents are divorced, so my aunt helped me and my brother with this process. To lose any parent is difficult. Even though it has been over 10 years since my dad has passed, I think about him often. No one can give you an estimated time on when your grieving process should be over. Everyone has a different relationship with each loved one. What works for me, may not work for you. What works for you may not work for me. There are two things that helped me; knowing that my dad and I had a great relationship and being reminded of God's love. Psalms 30:5 reads: "Weeping may endure for a night, but joy cometh in the morning". As my cousin would say, "But God".

December 11, 2020 is another Friday I will remember. My aunt, who was there when my dad passed, tackled cancer for as long as she could. She was a true warrior. She had been in remission, but when the cancer returned it was metastatic. The children and I spent a lot of weekends with her. She was a prayer warrior and a lady that truly walked as a follower of Christ. I miss my weekend visits and phone calls. She loved her family and it showed. It was hard seeing my other aunt have to go through the loss of her sister/best friend. They were extremely close. My surviving aunt did what she could in my aunt's battle against cancer. These two went to school together, traveled together, vacationed together. They even took their nieces and nephews on a few of those vacations. They were all about making memories and experiencing new things. They were about education and being prosperous spiritually and financially.

October 4, 2021

It's Monday. Thanking God for another day. The only thing I don't enjoy about getting ready for work is the hustle and urgency to get ready and be on time. Since I am here early, I decided to write before the bell rings.

My son's team played Thursday. I coach from the stands every game. As parents we get upset at games because we feel that the coaches are not doing what we think should be done. I am sure that coaching football is a lot more stressful than coaching cheer. Especially, when coaching older children.

We had a decent weekend. My husband seems OK. He isn't a walking ball of emotions like I used to be. On Saturday he worked around the house. I slept most of the day. Two of my nieces came to visit. My children have a great relationship with them. I enjoy it when I get the chance to visit with them.

Today I decided to reach out to the coach about game film for my son. Actually, I sent him a message yesterday but we had a face to face conversation today. One thing I know is that my children should know that their dad and I WILL ALWAYS support them and will stand up for them. My husband told me I was doing too much by talking to the coach, but I DON'T CARE. I AM MOM! James 4:2 reads: "Ye have not because ye ask not." I have prayed and I am pushing for my son to be successful academically and athletically.

October 5, 2021

Today is Tuesday. I woke up with the song *"Precious Lord"* on my mind. Sometimes when you're going through challenges, leaning on the Lord is the only relief you may get. Having a confidant helps as well. I am thankful for my family. There's no judgment passed, just sound advice given out of love. The five of my advisors are my heart (The Sixpack).

This morning on our way to the bus stop my son said he approaches football like a business. He stated that working out, doing drills, and watching films is the business side. He said being on the field playing the game is the exciting part. He mentioned that you get to let others see what your business is all about. I agree with every word he says. Psalms 37:4 says "Delight thyself also in the Lord; and He shall give thee the desires of thine heart." Prayerfully one day his desires will manifest.

October 8, 2021

Today is FRIDAY! I didn't go to the gym. I was super exhausted from work after the funeral yesterday. My son had a doctor's appointment. He is out of the cast and in a boot. He is SO EXCITED! He even started physical therapy today. Prayerfully God will keep his hands on him and keep him covered. 1 Peter 5:7 tells us to allow God to take care of our concerns. I stand and agree with my son that he will continue to have a healthy, yet speedy recovery. We are praying that he plays at least the last game. We are going to continue to work and pray. To God be the glory.

Have you ever just felt like nothing is working in your life?
(Journal your thoughts)

_____
_____
_____
_____
_____
_____
_____
_____
_____
_____
_____
_____
_____
_____
_____
_____
_____
_____
_____
_____
_____
_____
_____
_____
_____
_____
_____
_____
_____
_____

October 14, 2021

It's Friday Eve. So much has happened, but God. My cousin's husband was released from the hospital. My cousin is so strong. She has really been through so much, but yet remains faithful. There are six of us, we call ourselves "The SixPack".

My husband seems to be doing the best he can. He had the nerve to send us a message with a photo because our adorable, lovable, puppy keeps going in the trash on pickup day. I think he was just upset because he had to clean the trash up because it happened after we left for school. I told him when we put him on the leash, he gets off somehow. We put him in the kennel and he somehow finds a way to get the door opened enough to get out. My husband said he's Houdini. Houdini or not, he's just a pup.

October 17, 2021

Sunday, it's always a blessing to be among the living. I must say that I was feeling great and before noon I just started feeling hurt. Some things just don't seem as important to others as they may to you. I hate feeling this way. It feels bad because I try to be uplifting not just for me, but my family. I am not sure why I feel the way I do. I am not perfect by any means, but I try to do right by all. Lord please restore me, deliver me from this feeling.

October 22, 2021

    Today our football player went to the doctor. I know he's ready to get back to walking without any on that leg other than a sock and a shoe. His dad also has an appointment. I wish I could go with them both. I really think that my husband probably needs me more than my son does for his doctor's visit. My husband hasn't been to the doctor in a while.

    My daughter takes team pictures today. She really seems excited about the softball team! I am glad she is excited about some part of school. It is not the easiest thing to listen to her complain about school. She can't give me a valid reason as to why she doesn't like it. It's not like she's not liked or that she doesn't like her new classmates. The thing is that she's not with her friends that she's been in school with since elementary, that's my thought on it. I think she'll be just fine.

    Today my coworker decided to take a day off. He needs to. He is a real, live energizer bunny. One minute he's here, you look up and he's somewhere else before you can snap your fingers. I guess the students heard he'd be out so it seems that most of his homeroom was out. Maybe the students are out because they had a project due and need a little more time to complete it. I had one parent that gave me an excuse, that I know I probably will never hear again, as to why her child did not have his project. She reached out to me this morning before I made it to work. When she was talking in my mind I was saying, "Do you really expect me to believe this?" I guess she did since she called to tell me such an unbelievable story.

October 29, 2021

Our football player has been in his boot for two weeks. I still hurt for him because his excitement for this school year was like none other. This injury..........I am praying that whatever God does, he has favor over him. It gets harder and harder each week for him to see his team perform on the field.

I remember how my daughter felt when she broke her ankle. She couldn't go on the 7th grade Science field trip, she could no longer praise dance, and she THOUGHT she wouldn't be able to try out for cheer-leading. In April of 2020, she had signed up to try out for cheer-leading. I encouraged her to do so. I told her that they could see she had an ankle injury and that she just had to do what I had coached her to do over the past years (I am her former cheer-leading coach). With hard work, dedication, determination, and perseverance she made the squad.

My daughter has started wanting to go on dates. I have to remind her that she's 14 and that going to the movies once a month is one thing but we're not doing it every weekend or every other weekend. "Yes, I said we." She's upset because she thinks I'm being strict. WHATEVER! I hope she understands really soon what I am trying to teach her. If my words do not come across, she may need to have a conversation with her dad. I don't recall thinking about boys when I was 14. Let me not say that, because that was a long time ago.

How are your children (any friend or relative) that are in school dealing with COVID? Has this virus had an impact on their academics?
(Journal their experience)

Parenting can be a busted play. What are some of your parenting skills?
(Journal your skills)

November 7, 2021

Well it's Sunday. This is the first Sunday of the month. I haven't written in a while at home nor work. It seems that there's only enough time to WORK. There's so much going on, but there's no use in complaining because it seems that along with the complaints come more work.

My running back is no longer in a boot. He wears it when he has to work with his dad. He is excited to be wearing shoes. I'm excited to see him in two shoes. You know the one thing that aggravated me before his injury is the one thing I was missing, him running up and down the stairs. I promise it seemed like a herd of cows coming and going. He was not able to play the last game. I was hoping, well we were hoping that he would have been released from the doctor's care and been able to at least dress out. He can lift weights and get his upper body toned.

He texted me one day last week because of his academic slump. I told him it's not that he can't, he just needs to dedicate more time to his studies. He sometimes reminds me of Theo from the Cosby Show. I told him 20 minutes for each subject would be a good start, sometimes longer depending on the rigor of the subject. One more thing he doesn't do is ask us for help. He says we don't have patience. It's funny to hear him say that we don't have patience. I'm like, who taught you how to tie your shoes because you were crying in preschool because you couldn't tie them. I remember this day like it was yesterday. The teacher sent a note saying that he was really upset because he was not able to tie his shoes. Those shoes were special to him because he went with his dad to pick them out. That same evening, I taught him how to tie his shoelaces thanks to a video that showed a quick and sure proof method of how to tie shoelaces for toddlers. Who taught you how to regroup/carry when you were in the 2nd grade? I used his Hot Wheels to demonstrate the regrouping process. As a parent, I knew his interest and had to figure out some creative, out of the box way, to help him learn. Who taught you how to carry a football? Who taught you certain football drills when they had time off? Who taught you how to drill a bit? That would be Dad. When these children get older, I think they develop amnesia. He will get it together.

Now my daughter, she's cut from a different cloth. She feels that school should be Pre-K to 5th grade, skip middle school, then finish high school. She said you really learn what you need in the earlier years of school. She does just enough to not cause us to get on to her. I remember she used to be so competitive with her friends regarding academics. I think once she gets over the fact that she is remaining at her current school; she'll get her groove back.

I have told my children many times that all teachers will not go above and beyond. Some teachers do their job, no extra, and if the majority of the students understand, they move on. I think this is really true in middle and high school. Don't get me wrong, my children have/had teachers that go/went ABOVE and BEYOND. I told them it is just best to do the best they can at all times and ask questions if needed.

COVID has had an impact on education. When you're still overcoming being virtual/hybrid it is not easy. I think the children lost a lot, especially motivation to be in school. I know a lot of elementary students lost a lot. I think the teachers did as well because trying to keep any child at any age awake, engaged, and participatory was a task. It was more work teaching virtual, at least for me. Some students were assigned videos and just given assignments to complete. Did they learn anything? Some did and others probably didn't. God knows I honestly do not want to teach virtual. Shoot, it was hard for me to pay attention when I was the one teaching virtually.

When I'm in the classroom, I often find myself thinking about my children. How is their day going? Is the lesson being taught with excitement? Are they understanding? I know they are in high school, but they are still my priority. They are at the age where they say they don't need their parents; they have all the answers and solutions to their problems. I know that's a LIE. Sometimes children have to realize that success isn't just dependent upon them. Sometimes as parents we have to let our children fail so they can realize their plan isn't working and they have to be accountable. Now don't get me wrong, I don't want to see my children fail. I do want them to learn the lessons that their dad and I have taught them. When things don't go as they planned, I say "That was a bought lesson." They don't like when I tell them that!

We had a family meeting on Friday. Everyone expressed their concerns. We haven't really just sat down and had a conversation in a while. Sometimes we don't have conversations and tell how we feel, especially in African American families. I think we don't realize that the challenges are different for these children. I must say that sometimes the parenting in our household is not the best. It's like we're trying to mix old school with new school. On top of that, the children are on a different spectrum. One child just says "Yes ma'am", "Yes, sir." The other child says, "Well, why do I have to do it?" Sometimes I just want to SCREAM!

November 9, 2021

So on Sunday night, I didn't sleep worth anything. I'm not sure if it was the time change or the dream. This morning I woke up refreshed mentally. I feel like God was showing me something. Sometimes our problems are within and I wrestle with my thoughts daily. I feel God wants me to stop worrying so much and cast my cares on him 1 Peter 5:7 says: "Cast all your anxiety on him because he cares for us". I couldn't workout Monday (like I do sometimes) because even though I was refreshed mentally, I was tired physically. I barely had any energy. I am thankful that today is better than yesterday. I worry about my family. My children are in high school and I'm worried about how they are going to survive college. I have to remind myself that I can't see into the future and that in spite of all that has happened, God is going to protect them. Matthew 6:34 says " Take therefore no worry about tomorrow." I wish it was as easy to do as it is easy to read.

November 22, 2021

It has been a couple of weeks since I've written. Where do I begin? I think I'll start with my daughter. My daughter has started back complaining about school. She originally was going to attend school with her brother. Last week she mentioned to me that she has met some people, but it's just not the same as it was last year. I know it can be difficult to be at a new school and you may not know many people. If she was at school with her brother she'd know at least half of the students in her class and half in his class. I will say, she really likes her softball team and coaches. She talks about her head coach often. She said he's hard on them, but he is understanding and he listens. She has learned a lot more about softball which was the plan. In the district she attended, softball was not given much attention. Maybe they can't find coaches, maybe they think girls are not interested in the sport. The end of last school year, her dad mentioned about her transferring so that she could have the opportunity to play softball and learn all that she can.

Hopefully she'll understand why we made this decision and will see it through to the end. Sometimes sacrifices have to be made now so that you can enjoy the fruits of your labor later.

My son was not able to suit up for his last game because of his bone density. We are praying for the doctor to release him on his next visit next month. He is working out on his upper body. His dad and I are looking for someone to work with him on speed and agility. I know a personal trainer that I've taken boxing with that is experienced in speed and agility. This football season and school year has started out not as we had planned. I don't want any setbacks because he has endured enough, even while in my womb. I decided to speak with a counselor just to take precautions. The suggestions she provided were really helpful, journaling is one suggestion and being able to talk about our feelings. Journaling is something I've always done because it helps me to calm down and think through my problems. Thank goodness for God, because he listens and he knows and I don't have to worry about hearing what I said repeated by someone else. I believe God is going to give our son his moment to allow the world to see and know of his talents.

He is humble, confident, funny, and knowledgeable. I'm sure he's more than ready for another chance to get on the football field, but also ready to get on the soccer field.

My son recently met a friend. She seems really nice. He said she's smart and I think she plays almost every sport that a female can play. I've spoken with her a few times. His sister played softball with her, I think last year, and she said she's nice. Sisters can be hard on the "friend girls/girlfriends" just as us moms. Guess what, I have no problem with that because his sister is very cautious of who she calls "friend". She reads people. If she feels that something is wrong, she will say something to me. It doesn't matter if you're young or old.

Just a little prayer is mighty good to say, just a little prayer will help you on your way. Just a little prayer will bring you peace of mine, it's mighty good to say a prayer sometimes.

(Journal your prayer)

Merry Christmas! What was special about Christmas 2021?
(Journal your holiday experiences)

December 24, 2021

It's Christmas Eve. The weather is HOT! People are out last minute shopping and my son is out with his friend and her family. Her parents seem to be really nice as well as her siblings. They went to the movies, somewhere I haven't been in a while.

It's been a while since I've written. There are some good things going on. *GOD is GOOD!* On December 17, 2021 we took a trip to Atlanta to the *Black College National Championship*. It was a short trip, but a much needed good trip for the family. I thank my husband for planning the trip. He handled everything. It did my heart good to see all the smiles on my family's face. We had a good time, but my children were cutting up and are still making jokes. At the game, an older gentleman sat by me. I enjoy talking to older people. In conversing with him, I learned that he was at the game with his friends but because they all purchased tickets at different times, they all were in different sections of the stadium. We watched the game and were helping each other coach. Well, I took a selfie with him. My children had a fit! My son told me that if I cheat on his daddy, I'm cheating on the family. I told him to make sure to tell his dad the same thing. My daughter told me I was going to have to find a ride home. It was too funny! They were bugging their dad about this older gentleman sitting by me throughout the game. When we got in the truck I asked them what could I possibly do with someone old enough to be my father, possibly grandfather. My daughter had the nerve to say he's old enough to be a sugar daddy! What? How do you know about a sugar daddy?

The following Monday, December 20th, my son had his final appointment since his surgery. The doctor said his ankle has healed well. However, she wants him to wait maybe 5 weeks before he returns to his regular, athletic routine. He's excited! He has a dream and for a moment that dream has been placed on hold. Prayerfully his goals are aligned with the will of God.

    My daughter has been doing well. I allowed her to miss the last two days of school. She said they were only doing make-up work. I didn't want to force her and have to hear the complaining when she made it home. She has not been complaining about school. She is getting excited about the upcoming season. I think she is starting to embrace this change.

    I sent my aunt a message today because she's not coming home for Christmas. It is hard to know that she'll be alone this year. She and my other aunt spent Christmas together. My aunt assured me that she would not mope around tomorrow. She has friends that have invited her over, so maybe she'll take them up on their invitation. I can't imagine being so close to my sister and then realizing she's gone to never return, at least on Earth.

December 27, 2021

Well Christmas 2021 has come and gone. I feel that because of tradition we really never truly understand the reason we celebrate this day that has been set aside to acknowledge the birth of Jesus. There is so much to know and learn in the Bible. Sometimes we focus only on certain things in the Bible. I remember a deacon from my church back home once told me that he doesn't need to turn his TV set on because there was plenty of action that he NEEDED to know about in the Bible. Can't argue with that.

This Christmas was different. We've lost loved ones on my side and my husband's side of the family. The days past doesn't make it easier. The memories seem to come to the forefront of your mind. I spent the morning with my family and then went to my mom's. I really had a good time hanging out with my family in my hometown. I had the chance to see my other niece and nephew. We talked, laughed, slept, ate, talked some more, and laughed some more. My husband and the children spent the day with his side of the family. I'm sure this was a difficult time for them as well. I think he needed the children to be with him. I know they are not babies, but sometimes you can just imagine. Sometimes being with the children can be a good distraction of what's going on. Both of my children know how to get you laughing.

Happy New Year! (Journal your plans for 2022)

January 4, 2022

    Today we didn't do anything. Well, the children and I didn't do anything. My husband had to punch the clock. I went to the gym this morning. I try so hard to be on time, but it is so hard letting go of the bed. It seems like it takes me longer to get ready for the gym than it does for work. I had a great workout! When I made it home, I just relaxed. Once my daughter got up we watched a few Netflix movies. We were in my room, sitting up in bed. She told me that I needed to calm down. She said I act just like my mom. Whatever! My mom wants to watch the movie, but if she knows you've watched it she wants you to tell her about it. She will ask a million and one questions while watching. Sometimes I don't tell her that I've watched a movie. When my daughter wants to hang out with me I take her up on it because she's like a hermit and stays shut up in her room. I must say, during the winter break she hung out with me a lot.

January 5, 2022

Happy 17th birthday, my son! Last night we sat and talked and laughed about the times gone by. I can remember when I found out I was pregnant. I went to the doctor because my foot was causing me pain. I had to take a routine pregnancy test, you know the rest! I was excited and afraid at the same time. I was excited because we were pregnant and afraid because we had miscarried before.

He talked about the times in his younger days that he remembered. He mostly remembered the toys that were his favorites: Nerf, wrestling men figures, Hot Wheels, basketballs and footballs. He even remembers the first basketball team he played on when he was 4, the Grizzlies. I told him about the days his dad would come home from work in the mornings and would come immediately to hold him. I told him about the days his dad would play with him on the floor once he started crawling. He remembers being outside with his dad all the time. He ran everywhere then and does now!

My son feels that we're changing how we parent. I had to remind him that as he got older, our approach to parenting changed because we are raising a boy that we want to continue to be a servant of God, a humble young man, a productive young man, a respectful, loving young man. Proverbs 22:6 read: "Train up a child in the way he should go and when he is old he will not depart from it." I explained it and he said he understands. We'll see in a few years! Of course, he thinks his dad is too hard (sometimes, maybe, maybe not). He thinks I'm overly protective and overbearing.(sometimes, maybe, maybe not).

I tell both my children that if they ever have a family of their own, they'll recognize the challenges. They will see what their dad and I were talking about. They will see themselves in their children and will probably be calling us 24-7. My daughter is going to just look at them and tell them to go to their rooms. My son is probably going to give them a story based upon an experience he has had and try to get them to understand. This is what their dad currently does. I remember a few months ago when we had our family talk my husband showed the kids a clip of a movie that Denzel Washington played in. In the movie, Denzel played this dad who had a teenage son. Denzel asked the son why he thinks he did the things he did as his father? Denzel answered his own question by saying, "It was his responsibility."

    Well, that's not what the children felt should have been the response. They felt that Denzel being the dad should have responded that he does what he does because he loves his son. He probably should have used a different movie to get this point across.

    Today was also a big day for other reasons as well. I had to have a digital mammogram. I had my annual checkup last week and they found a spot in my left breast. My doctor called me and told me the news, I was speechless. I cried! I called my husband and started crying. I called my mom and cried again. I texted my cousins and told them. I called my aunt and cried. Sometimes we hold things in without sharing, but you have to know who to share with. I needed someone to pray for me. Sometimes others have gone through what you're going through and can help along the way. Due to COVID there are no visitors allowed in the doctor's office. My husband could have gone to work, but he sat in his truck at the doctor's office. He didn't complain about having to wait; he just wanted to be there. I didn't think I could be more in love with him, but this moment proved me wrong. After the imaging, the doctor gave me the good news to let me know that everything was fine. He said he knows that I probably was a mental mess. Yes, I was! As my cousin would say, "But God." He is always working before we even get a plan together.

 This morning before my appointment, I went to the gym. I had the opportunity to wear a mock-up workout attire that my cousin designed. When I say that I am super excited for her. She has always been an entrepreneur. Her mind is constantly working. She asked me a few months ago about wearing one of her pieces. I couldn't say no! I just picked it up on Tuesday. I sent her pictures of me wearing it once I made it home. I sent her my reviews today. I hope I'm a little slimmer the next time I wear it. I told her that I would give another review after I've washed it and worn it again.

January 6, 2022

Well today my plan to actually publish my book may become reality. I met with my consultant tonight. Oh my goodness! She provided me with so much information. There are so many resources available for new authors. She had me thinking that I could be the next best selling author. I know that it is possible and I pray that my experience helps someone else. She has provided me with deadlines and some suggestions for my book. I am so excited and anxious! This is something that I have wanted to do for so long. Who knows, this may give birth to my talk show *"Let's Talk, Real Talk"*.

The break is over! How was your first day back after your time off?
(Journal about your day)

January 7, 2022

I went to the gym this morning. Child, I'm done. I need to lose some of this weight before my next doctor's visit. I've been at this challenge for 14 years. I do good, fall off, do descent, fall, off. It's just back and forth; up and down.

My daughter's first day back to school was Tuesday. She has not complained about school. She has said that practice and school has been going well. I'm going to hope that we keep this same positive attitude. She received her grades and said she was going to push for straight A's. We'll see!

Yesterday was my students' first day back. My homeroom class was eerily quiet. Not saying that they are just loud and rambunctious. They are just a lively crew. I must say that it wasn't a bad day at work. After work, I picked my daughter up from school. She complains about having to ride the bus in the evening because she said there are too many children on the bus and she does not want to get COVID. I had to remind her to just do her part and stay masked up. I picked up my son from the bus stop. He called me six times. I was busy doing things around the house after I picked his sister up from school. I told him he now sees how his dad and I feel when we call or text and he doesn't respond; rather intentional or not.

The biggest loser....what are some things you've had to release so that you could refocus?
(Journal about your release)

January 9, 2022

Well, today starts a 90 day weight loss challenge. It starts off with a challenge, detoxing for ten days. The trainer that I go to now, we had great talk last. She understands what I'm going through because she has been there before. She is a great support line to have. Now that I have accepted this challenge, I need to be mentally prepared. Really, the only thing that satisfies my cravings is some sweets. Since I had COVID last February, my taste buds are not what they used to be and I can only smell smoke, sometimes. Now I have this weight loss challenge, a challenge at work, the children and their academics, work (because I've been asked to teach up a grade), marriage(need to maintain a healthy relationship), and my salvation to work on this year. I am not going to allow myself time to put my thoughts into someone else's business unless they ask. This year is truly going to be the year for me to focus on those that are near and dear to me. I've gotten off social media for a while because I was spending so much time doing that when I could have been reading the Bible more, a good book, spending time with the family, or just resting. Shut, this time I plan to give my attention to what is in front of me. I have a lot of work to do on myself.

Ten days into the new year, how's it going?
(Journal about your first ten days)

January 10, 2022

Monday, the beginning of another work week. Today, I meal prepped for the challenge. I know it started Sunday, but I wasn't ready mentally. It takes a lot of mental focus to lose weight and to work out.

I didn't sleep too well last night. One reason is because the dogs kept barking. Seemed like every time I dozed off, they'd start barking. Another reason is that when I finally drifted off to sleep, my husband busted up in the room like the police turned the lights on, why I have no clue. It's not like he didn't know I was in the bed sleeping, or trying to sleep. He was literally in the bedroom for 10 seconds before he went into the bathroom. Basically he just walked through the bedroom to get to the bathroom. I heard him running the water, mind you, the light is still on in the bedroom. I had to get up to turn the lights off. I was pissed! Once he was out of the bathroom, he didn't turn the lights on. That leads me to believe you didn't need the lights anyway. With all that went on last night, I was basically napping.

Because of my napping, I made it to the gym on time. Getting up to be somewhere before 5 a.m. that doesn't pay you is a challenge. The workout was good. The trainer is always pushing and being so encouraging. Sometimes she calls my name because I will take a break at any given moment. When I'm getting tired, I'll scream "Joy!" or "Child!" These are the words I choose instead of some other choice words. Oftentimes, I just look at her in disbelief because of her workout request, but she makes it fun but it doesn't change the fact that "I BE TIED!"

January 15, 2022

Happy birthday Momma and Dr. King! This has been a tiresome week. Lord, I do thank you for this journey. Work has not been so bad. My class is still quiet. I moved my comedian to another class because he has been performing so well. I do miss the entertainment and I think the students in my homeroom do as well. On yesterday, I shed one or two tears because one of my students is relocating. I was not prepared for such news!

I've been assigned a new task at work, co-teaching up a grade. I must admit, I let the administrator know that I will do whatever I can within reason to help the students. I mention that I am there to assist and to not take over. I hope that this is helpful as it concerns the students. I want them to learn as much as they can while having fun. I want this to be a fun and learning experience for me and my coworker as well. I remember how it was when I taught first, co-teaching was fun

So this weightloss challenge; well, I'm actually in two challenges now. There's one at work and one at the gym. The work challenge is to see who is going to lose the most weight and win the pot of money. The gym challenge is on a whole different level! You have to detox for a period of time, spend a certain amount of time in the gym, and do certain exercise challenges. I must admit, I'm doing good so far. This detox is for the birds though! You have to meal prep to stay on track, I'm on it. I have a few more days remaining to detox and I have worked out 3 days this week.

The gym challenge, I also had to send in pictures. Let me just say that sometimes I don't want to see what's under these clothes, but to share with others, OMG! To help me be more aware of my body, I purchased waist beads.

Obviously, I should have had someone to tie them on because I had beads all in the bed and the floor the first night I tied them. Out of 3 beads one is fully beaded. I'm basically walking around with 2 strings and 1 waist bead. Oh well.

January 16, 2022

Sunday mornings, what a blessing. Church is still limited in capacity. I didn't attend in person service, but attended virtual. This morning, I only received teaching from my normal second service. The message was, "Things are gonna happen sooner than you expect". There are many things I've prayed for that I hope the Lord allows to happen sooner.

Last night my daughter and I watched a couple of movies. I am really enjoying this time she wants to spend with me. She says I annoy her sometimes when we're watching movies because I do a lot of narrating. We watched a great animation movie last night, and she cried. To my surprise, I didn't. The movie is called "*Riverdance*". After the movies, she baked a red velvet cake. She really enjoys baking. She mentioned doing some baking on the side. I'm down for a good hustle!

My son had a wonderful birthday surprise last night. His girlfriend, his best friend, and her best friend surprised him for his birthday and took him to dinner. They couldn't make it last weekend so this was a great way to celebrate and this was a great way to show true friendship.

My husband worked yesterday. When he made it home, he opted not to sit up and watch the movie with me and our daughter. He decided to watch football instead. I'm really not interested in the playoffs now since my team is out, the Baltimore Ravens.

January 23, 2022

Well, today is the start of a new week. I accomplished a lot last week. God has really been amazing. There's been cold weather, rainy weather, and just the type of weather where you just want to cuddle up with a blanket and watch some **Golden Girls**.

Work the past week has been exhausting. It seems when there's a shorter week, it requires more because it seems as if there's not a lot of time to finish anything. I co-taught with my co-worker today. I really enjoyed it. It's good to collaborate and be able to motivate others that have the same goals and interests and they in turn motivate you. My 4th grade students love it. The 5th grade students are adjusting. They realize that I am nice, but I take my job seriously which means they are required to give their best. The students are being pushed to think on a higher level..

My 4th grade team members are doing their things. We are on different spectrums, but we really want the best for the students. One is really relaxed, loud and busy. One is structured, organized, and passionate. Me on the other hand, I'm somewhere in the middle. I like structure, but not too much because I am quick to get off task. I'm relaxed, but not too relaxed because I don't want the students to feel like I'm their friend. I feel that the three of us have the same goal, educate our students so they can be successful in the future.

My daughter had to go to urgent care on Thursday. When the nurse called me from the school, I was like, "What now?" We can't afford another injury. Praise God it was just a pulled muscle. Hopefully, she'll be ready by Wednesday to practice. As the medical mother, she is stiff and moving slowly, but she'll be ok.

My son is working in school, as he should. I see a good difference. He was a little down on Wednesday when I picked him up. He wasn't talking 90 to nothing. I figured it out after we got home. The regional team roster was released and I'm positive that it just brought a lot of "ifs" for him. I didn't mention it and he didn't bring it up.

My husband has started working out. He said he needs my waist beads. I told him that it would be funny if he was bent over and beads were seen on him. Now yesterday when he came home, it was not so funny. He was all puffed up, not sure why. Maybe it was the hot dogs overcooking on the stove. I couldn't smell them because I don't have a sense of smell. The children were in their rooms. I honestly forgot they were on the stove because I started doing something else. On top of that, he had the nerve to ask me what had I been doing all day. Well sir, if you must know, I showered, put on my lounge wear, did laundry, and made sure you all had chili dogs and fries to eat. I don't know what he thought I was supposed to be doing.

February 6, 2022

Well there's so much that happened that I just didn't see coming. Sometimes I feel like I'm running a losing race. Just when those thoughts begin to appear, God shows up with a message from my cousin. I really enjoy talking to her. We seem to have similar concerns. Next weekend I've scheduled a photo shoot for the family. I've been so mentally occupied with other things in life that for a moment I forget about my personal project. I honestly don't know if I'm going to finish this project. There's football training after school, softball practice after school with the season starting in a week or so, soccer practice, and the pressures of work.

My son has started training to help get back in shape, get faster and to increase his endurance. He seems to enjoy it and I'm glad he gets along with his trainer. I knew he would because this young man is young, talented, and patient.

What are your thoughts on education in the 21st century?
(Journal your thoughts)

February 10, 2022

It sometimes seems like when you give your all, it's just not enough. Being in education is a job that you are not compensated enough for. You come early, only to leave late. No one forces you, but it's needed because there's such a demand for teachers. I remember when I was in grade school, my teachers seemed to really enjoy what they did. It seemed as if they were given the opportunity to teach "reading, writing, and arithmetic" their way. If students were taught the way we were, we wouldn't have to do all these things. Children are in upper elementary and do not know multiplication facts. Let's be real, parents didn't wait on the teacher to teach you the alphabet, how to count, how to pronounce and spell your first and last name, address, and birthday. I'm just stating the facts of what I remember. I knew the majority of what I needed to know in first grade while in Head Start. Now, some people don't believe early childhood learning is necessary. It was necessary in my parent's house and it was necessary in our house. What do I know?

On top of work, I'm dealing with my neighbor about our puppy. I think we finally have a solution to the drama. He has gotten in their trash again. He loves it because it's so easy to get to. I know he shouldn't go through the trash, but dogs are like people;curious. If their trash is destroyed, they can't blame him. There's more I'd like to say, but I'll say this, as an adult don't approach a child (especially one that doesn't know you) about an issue that should be discussed with an adult.

I Can't Quit
(Journal your thoughts)

February 13, 2022

This morning me and my husband attended church. The service was really good. Our daughter would have been uncomfortable the entire time. She is still cautious when it comes to being around a lot of people inside. Yes, she attends school and rides the bus. She disinfects and it gets on her classmates' nerves. I can't be mad with her. She tells us often that if she could be virtual she would. That's not happening, even if it was an option because she gets distracted easily and loves to sleep like me.

The subject for the sermon today was "I can't quit". It came from 2 Corinthians 4:7-9. I could really relate to this subject because there have been many times I've wanted to quit. The thought has come and gone in so many areas of my life. God always gives a reminder, Ecclesiastes 9:11- The race is not given to the swift or to the strong, but to the one who endures to the end. Today's message is just what I needed to remind myself to finish the project that I've started.

When you think you're done, but you realize there's more to be done.
(Journal your thoughts)

February 19, 2022

Well, today is Saturday and I thought I was finished writing. Life said, "No". If there was a way to capture all the good and just sprinkle it upon each individual across this world, this would be a better place. One of my favorite verses Matthew 5:16 reads, "Let your light shine before me, that they may see your good works and glorify your Father which is in heaven." Sometimes the enemy tries to dim that light.

Let me see if I can gather my thoughts from the week. Monday the students didn't have to attend school because of parent-teacher conferences and professional development. I must say the conferences went well. I had the opportunity to meet parents that I haven't met in the two years I've taught my students. Tuesday the students returned and for the most part, did what was expected of them. My daughter had her first high school game! What a great way to a season opener with a JV win and Varsity win!

Wednesday was a day for all of us in education and parents. There was an incident that happened and it just was so hurtful to hear. I was told about it during class and I immediately texted my son because when you hear certain things, your mind just starts racing. He responded back that he was OK, but the events that occurred had him feeling some type of way. Even today, I'm thinking about what happened. When I picked him up from school, he shared with me his thoughts about what happened on Wednesday. I told him I didn't have all that answers, but I assured him that they would get to the bottom of the situation. Everyone had their thoughts about what happened, but one of my church members posted that we shouldn't say anything crazy about the situation and don't place blame, but just pray. I responded," Sometimes we forget that children are people too. These children have way much more to deal with than we did at their age. Sometimes they feel as if they can't talk to anyone because they feel as if what is said in confidence will be repeated." FACTS! When my daughter made it in from school she had questions about the situation as well. Children need someone they can talk to and feel comfortable and safe with. I have a village that consists of people that we don't mind speaking with our children. I'm thankful that I can just text or call the counselor and she makes herself available.

Thursday, I received a text about another situation and I was just speechless. Being a parent it is hard dealing with certain matters that may affect your children especially when you can't be there. I constantly pray over my children. I always ask for covering and protection from dangers seen and unseen. To help ease the tension, my sister-in-law checked him out of school. After that I was at ease and she decided to get my daughter and my nieces and they went to Prentiss to attend our uncle's viewing.

Friday, we didn't attend work or school. We attended our uncle's funeral in Silver Creek. It was good seeing our family, but not under the circumstances. I didn't spend much time in Silver Creek after the funeral. I decided to go to Monticello to visit my mom since I haven't seen her since December. We talk almost every day on the phone, at least two or three times. Family is everything to me! Without my family I don't think I could have made it through the past two years. Let's see what life has for us next. I pray that whatever comes my way that I have the strength to endure and that the Lord keeps his loving arms of protection around not just me, but each of us.

www.ingramcontent.com/pod-product-compliance
Lightning Source LLC
Chambersburg PA
CBHW052121110526
44592CB00013B/1697